LISTEN UP, BLACK GIRL

SYDNEY WASHINGTON

SMS WRITE ON PUBLISHING, LLC.

Copyright © 2021 by Sydney Washington

All rights reserved.

No part of this book may be reproduced in any form or by any electronic or mechanical means, including information storage and retrieval systems, without written permission from the author, except for the use of brief quotations in a book review.

ISBN 978-1-7355437-4-1

"To Mom and Brianne, who saw the worst in me and they still believe I am phenomenal."

CONTENTS

1. Hey, black girl — 1
2. Be strong, black girl — 6
3. Destroy a black girl — 11
4. Caged, black girl — 18
5. Misfortune of a black girl — 27
6. Shameful black girl — 34
7. The "strong" black girl — 38
8. Boundaries of the black girl — 41
9. Heal, black girl — 44
10. Let them See you Cry — 52

1

HEY, BLACK GIRL

If you're reading this, I want you to know that we are beautiful. From the way our hair grows wild and in the direction of the sun, down to the last drop of melanin on our toes. Beautiful and worth every bit of a lovely life. Sometimes we go through experiences that attempt to dim the way we shine. I'm here to tell you that no matter what, don't let anyone make you feel less than who you are.

Take me, for example, if someone would have warned me that I would suffer many heart breaks, maybe I wouldn't have beaten myself up about the way I coped with things. No one's ever told me that sad feelings were normal or that it was okay to talk about them. The thing about trauma is that these emotions surrounding it sit like stains on you until the day you decide to wash them off. You gotta learn to heal, girl.

As a young black woman, I had to learn what baggage was mine to carry versus what other people chose to put on me. Even though I should not have had to, I somehow carried it all, anyway. I felt like I had to prove I was strong and could handle whatever life threw at me. Then one day, the burden became too big to carry any more. That's right, I nearly lost my damn mind.

I checked myself into a mental facility for the sake of saving my family from embarrassment. To be honest, I've been ready to give up so many times. Many black women don't admit these things, but let me be the one to tell you, the story keeps getting uglier if you let it. Sometimes we just continue through life without handling our mess, we just get through it because we're expected to.

It wasn't until I was in therapy for the third time that I realized I had the overwhelming need to please people. I wanted everyone to accept me, to love me. All the time I said yes to favors for others, even when it inconvenienced me or made me uncomfortable. I had this desperate need to show up for others and it didn't matter what feelings I had surrounding it. I always said yes. I later learned this was from growing up, being the child of a single mom.

I remember saying to myself when I was in elementary school, "If I get good enough grades, mommy will be proud of me." Very rarely did she ever show up to my award ceremonies in between graduations, so I'll always remember that hunger inside of me that pushed me to excel in school with hopes that I'd see her cheering in the crowd. I had adopted the need to please others as some sort of an unsigned contract of acceptance. I was always there for others, even when it felt like no one was there for me.

As an adult, I now understand that as a single mother, she worked so much because she had to financially support four children. She spent a lot of time away from us. Like most strong black women, my mother was a hard worker, because she had to be. Her children relied on her and ultimately, she was the first role model in our lives. No matter how hard our situation got, I never saw her cry. So naturally, neither did I. Tears were a sign of weakness. She always found a way to just figure it out. This was how I learned many of my life-changing lessons. I was an observer; I took life in through my eyes and tried to make sense of it in my head as I saw fit.

Because I've seen a lot of things in my early years, I was wiser than I should have been for my age. Looking back at my experiences, I didn't know that this would be the beginning of an emotional roller coaster that would last for most of my adolescent and early adult years. I would often find myself spinning out of control with overwhelming anger and then later picking up the pieces of whatever destruction I had caused. I would then go back to my normal self, pretending to have life all figured out, and then I'd be spiraling all over again. Whether it was my friends, family, or myself, someone would always be hurt at the end of my rampage.

Now, don't go on thinking I grew up to be an angry adult because I didn't have enough attention as a child. The point is, throughout my journey in life, I had to learn a lot of lessons on my own. This included making some terrible decisions at the time and learning that I shot myself in the foot later. I also endured some deep wounds that I'm deciding to rip the band aid off, to take the super woman cape off and tell you about so that you can help break the cycle. Black women deserve to be soft and vulnerable too.

Trauma isn't always recognized at first and we definitely wouldn't dare speak about it for whatever reason as a child. Is it because we aren't taught to speak up? Had someone scared us into not telling? Had we forgotten about the trauma because it was too much to bear at the time? I can't speak the same reasons for everyone, but for me, I didn't recognize or know that the people you expect to love you can also be the same ones that will hurt you the most.

2

BE STRONG, BLACK GIRL

As black women, we are often described as strong, the people who just get things done. No matter what it may cost, we find a way to make the impossible happen. I'm not talking about statistics or anything. I'm just speaking from experience and what I have witnessed growing up.

If I could give a description to the "Strong Black Woman", I would say she is nurturing, brave, reliable, and most importantly, a legacy maker. More often than not, black women were the head of the household in my hometown. She was the breadwinner and the homemaker, the person who passed her way of life from generation to generation. She has emotional restraint, while taking on multiple roles and continues to care for others. The strong black woman faces obstacles with whatever resources she has. She tackles stress in her own way, and she doesn't ask for help.

Asking for help would mean she was a failure. She couldn't handle it, she wasn't strong enough. Maybe she didn't have anywhere to turn and ask for help to begin with. Because she didn't want to be called weak, she stuck it out. By any means, she will figure it out. Being the legacy-maker has come with big shoes to fill. No one wants to let down everyone around you, especially not the strong black woman. High expectations she shall meet by any means because she has to.

She continues to fight the battle, even if she has to fight it alone. That's what you do when you're strong. You fight and you continue to fight no matter what, because one day, you want to be able to say you made it.

I often think about when slavery was present and what it would have been like for a black woman during that time. I imagine she was not able to cry about the tragedies that happened to her. Trauma naturally built up inside of her and her family, with no way to release itself. They endured immeasurable amounts of violence, trauma, and rape.

Still today, these same trauma responses are

being passed down from generation to generation to black girls to develop the skills necessary to survive an existence of violence, hypersexulization and other forms of trauma. We are still nursing our wounds with the same mindset and healing pattern. That's just it, we aren't healing from our traumas as we journey through life to adulthood. Traumatic memories resurface and they become the thing that defines our character. How we coped or dealt with things that happened to us dictate how we handle stress as adults.

I've seen pent up stress and trauma turn into mental illness and unstable behavior for myself. I became an adult who did not know how to deal with situations that made me uncomfortable. I wouldn't stand up for myself when it was most important. I had low self-esteem, and I realized I was pouring all my issues into the hearts of my children. How was I going to raise functioning black men? If I didn't take care of myself first, there was no way I was going to raise my children right. I don't want them growing up with a false sense of masculinity because I have a warped sense of femininity.

I was teaching them to be angry, just like me. To yell and fight their emotions, instead of listening to what their souls were trying to communicate to them. I was a stranger to my emotions and reacted to life the only way I knew how, in silence. The silence manifested into dark feelings and actions. Actions like physically and mentally abusing myself. That's when I recognized it was time to make a change. I needed to break the generational curse of my family.

I wanted to continue carrying the reputation of being strong and resilient as other black women had, but I realized I was doing it all wrong. How was I going to remain that way if I wasn't doing anything but staying silent? What was I doing to remain strong and resilient? I'm pointing this out because we, as black women, need to recognize when it's time to come back and be nurturing to ourselves as we often are to other people.

Eventually, everyone has their breaking point. Even the strong black woman. She doesn't share her failures with the world, not even those closest to her. It makes a hell of a battle inside her mind. Does she give up? How does she keep fighting? When does she speak up?

If someone had taught me how to be more gentle with myself, maybe I would have. That is why I am writing this book. To tell you, "Listen up, black girl, it's time to speak up". It's time to heal from the things that happened to you and the things that happened to others that they placed on you. So you can be your best self.

3

DESTROY A BLACK GIRL

When I was six years old, I went to daycare while my mother worked. I remember being molested at an overnight sleepover by the daycare provider's son. He was very much older than I was at the time, in his teens. I was wearing a pink and purple onesie. Most of my memory consisted of pain physically and emotionally that spiraled me out of control for years to follow.

I never shared my secret with anyone about what happened. I didn't know that it would manifest into emotional pain and that I would act it out through hypersexuality. No matter what I did, I was still unsatiated. Touching myself didn't cure the disease and letting him continue did not make it go away either. I knew I always felt uncomfortable, but I didn't know what to do about it. It was just something I happened to get used to. I felt this darkness inside me. No one ever noticed anything was wrong. I don't remember my parents having the "No one should ever touch you" conversation and weren't around enough to check in with me about if someone had actually done it.

This was the first time I had mistrust in the males that were present in my life. I didn't think that they would all hurt me, but I didn't believe that they truly loved me, either. When I became older, I mistrusted my relationships with the guys I was dating. I believed as long as I gave them what they wanted, we'd stay together. I didn't date a lot of guys, but the ones that I did only showed me I wasn't ready for any genuine relationships. I felt that love would only be felt if it were given in some sort of exchange. I didn't know what real love was, let alone real self love.

I guess this also comes from not having a close relationship with my father because my parents weren't together and he lived out of state. We didn't talk much when we weren't visiting him. When my sister and I did visit, he was also working a lot, like my mother. Naturally, I had no idea what the love of a father really felt like because we did not form a close bond. They say a daughter's first love is her father, well I was cheated out of that part of life.

I felt unsure of myself growing up. I always had this feeling that I was missing something. I didn't feel completely empty inside, but I had this longing that was beginning to fester. I wanted to feel loved and accepted. I didn't know I was hurting inside. Pain did not feel like pain. This felt different. I felt left out, especially because my half sister was living with my father. She got to spend most of her life getting to know the stranger I called "Daddy". I felt like she had the perfect childhood, while my sister and I barely knew him.

I was mentally mature for my age and had to be because while my mom was at work; I helped with my siblings a lot. I would make sure that the house was clean by the time she came home and would help my siblings get ready for school by the time she came home from work in the mornings while my step dad was sleeping. I would often babysit my youngest sister. We were ten years apart. Once, I remember taking her outside to play when she was about two or three. Some adult asked me was she my daughter? I was so confused as to why someone would ask me if my sister was my daughter. Didn't I look like a kid to them?

As the years went by and I had reached my preteen stage, men and women began to look at me differently. They talked bad about me when they thought I wasn't listening. They would make negative comments and fortune tell my future about how my hips were spreading, and it could only mean one thing. "She's going to be a handful when she gets older", a comment I remember hearing as I walked by a group of adults talking. I may have forgotten who said it, but I definitely remember those words. I didn't know what it meant until grown men, well men in general, started making inappropriate passes at me.

I was eleven years old, walking to the corner of my street to get something from the store. That's when the first advancement was made. The neighborhood drunk grabbed my arm and kissed the side of my neck. It was the first time I had ever smelled beer on someone's breath. I can still feel the wetness on my neck when I think about it sometimes. I felt gross and violated.

I used to pour my heart out to my best friend. We

met in eighth grade. He was the new student, and I was the first person to befriend him. One day we exchanged numbers and that started the daily routine we had. We were weird. We ignored each other during the school day, but as soon as we got home, we'd rush to the phone and tell each other all about what happened that day. We were in different classrooms, so pretending to be strangers was easy.

He slowly began to develop a crush on me, which lasted throughout most of high school. I hadn't entirely felt the same way he felt. After all, he was my best friend. I enjoyed the friendship we had, and I wasn't ready to change it.

I went over to his house one day after a date. I was sixteen years old at the time and a friend of my mom's son had asked for me to join him at the movies. After the movie was over, he sent me a text saying he had a girlfriend all along and he shouldn't have gone to the movies with me in the first place.

I wanted to gossip and vent, so I hopped off the bus and found myself at my best friend's. I had been there a few times, and we had always laughed about dates with people and enjoyed catching up. It was a second home to me. I remember one time, his father let me in while he wasn't home. Ridiculously, I thought it was a great idea to take the condoms in his room and blow them up like balloons. I hid them all around his closet, between his clothes, in shoe boxes, all kinds of places.

Anyway, I wanted to tell my best friend about one of the most embarrassing dates I had been on. We sat on his bed and we laughed about how my date was a complete fail. Then the look in his eyes changed. He kept staring at my jeans. At that moment, he asked for me to take them off. I was immediately disturbed by his request. He decided to remove them himself. The latch broke, and so did my heart. When it was over, I sat up. Tears welled up in my eyes. I got up, got dressed, and ran. I ran all the way home. I held those tears until my face crashed into my pillow on my bed. My best friend has taken advantage of me. Out of all the men in my life, I was betrayed by my best friend. Years of trust and secrets spilled from my mind. If I couldn't trust him, who was I going to trust?

When speaking about my story now, people often ask "Well, why didn't you tell anyone what he did to you?". Before I didn't have an explanation, however now I see that I was used to men showing me I couldn't trust them. I could have told my step brothers and let them decide how to handle it, however that didn't feel like a good enough solution.

I also did not want to go through the court system, and this was someone I had trusted for years. I struggled with it for a long time. No decision would have made the amount of emotional turmoil that I was feeling inside of me go away.

4

CAGED, BLACK GIRL

In middle school, I was very self-conscious about how I looked. We went to a bilingual elementary school, where a lot of the other children were of Spanish descent. I would tell them I was mixed with whatever they were so I wouldn't get made fun of for being "just black". I wanted lighter skin, and I didn't think those darker than me were pretty. I was made fun of for not having long hair and because of the shape of my lips.

I was typically the last one picked for dating and usually broken up with for a girl that I felt was prettier than me. I was teased for the clothes I was wearing because they weren't name branded and my sneakers weren't what everyone was wearing.

This was around the time I would start starving myself so that I did not gain too much weight, because adults would make comments and say I was going to be "thick". To me, that meant fat. It took a long time for me to learn to love the skin that I was in. I would wear clothes that covered up as much as possible. I felt uncomfortable in dresses most of the time. I didn't have much of a selection of clothes, so I would often trade with the friends who weren't in the same schools as me, so no one would know.

I was thirteen when my father told me I didn't need to think about boys or even like them. I had tried to tell him about a boy I had a crush on at camp. He cut me off mid-sentence. It had hurt my feelings at the time because I didn't even understand the emotions I was feeling. I just wanted to tell someone about it. So I stopped sharing secrets with him. I decided to keep my experiences to myself.

I dreaded telling him I was pregnant for the first time at nineteen years old. I always felt like I needed to make him proud of me. That I was doing a good job with life. So when I learned I was pregnant, I had many mixed emotions. Would my dad support me? Would he be happy? I guess I was just going to have to get over my thoughts and just tell him.

My father was not happy about it, in fact his

response was "People have the right to choose if they want to be grandparents or not." Although he said it out of anger, I knew he was going to have to accept it. I didn't understand what he meant by that until our fragile relationship became even more estranged. We didn't speak much after that and he didn't show up to my baby shower months later. He didn't even show up to my wedding two years after I had my first son. I remember him texting me, saying he didn't think it was a good idea that he'd come. No explanation, just that he wasn't coming.

The words exchanged between my father and I during those years brought some dark feelings out of me. They were strong, and the intention behind them was to cause pain. I was becoming more short-tempered and angry as the years went by. I didn't feel good enough. I felt damaged, and that I had messed up my life even more because I had a child at a young age. That I wasn't going to be a good mother. I hadn't even finished college yet. I felt like I was going to be a failure for the rest of my life.

I'd have these episodes of explosive anger. I was just angry about things I couldn't put a reason to. I shut myself in my room for days, barely eating. Sleepless nights were a part of my routine and when I slept, nightmares were present.

I stopped caring how I looked and didn't want to hang out with friends. The ones I did hang with I got into arguments and said things to them that they shouldn't have forgiven me for. My own family said I was becoming hard to deal with. My relationships with everyone began to suffer due to my own destruction.

My only sense of happiness was my son. He knew when I was sad or when I was angry and the sight of him would immediately calm me down. Then I would beat myself up inside because I felt like I wasn't being a good mother. I was supposed to be happy all the time in his presence. When he saw me cry or have angry outbursts, I felt ashamed. How could I lose control in front of an innocent and pure child? Instead of showing my weakness, I would hold it in and continue to show him how strong I was, no matter what happened. I had to be strong for Mateo.

At the time, I was too ignorant to recognize that I needed help dealing with my traumas that were starting to resurface. I was no longer the sweet and kind person everyone loved. I was harsh and violent in my relationship with my boyfriend. Arguments often resulted in others needing to intervene or police visits to the house.

I remember a time when Mateo was young and his father and I were just getting used to becoming new parents. We had just finished being intimate, and he began to get ready. When I asked him where he was going, his response was that he had dinner with a female friend whose parents she wanted him to meet. I was speechless. I silently watched him get ready to go to dinner and left. Once I gathered what he had told me, I broke down and sat on the floor, crying. I cried so hard that my body began to shake and I couldn't breathe. Mateo was six weeks old at the time. I grabbed him out of the bassinet and held him as I cried. I couldn't breathe, and my head was pounding. What a way to break up with me. From that moment on, I vowed never to cry again over a breakup. Another trauma was born within me.

Racing thoughts crowded my head from time to time. Irrational ideas lead to irrational actions. Suicide ideation became a popular thought for me. Worthlessness was at the top of the list for things I felt. I was later diagnosed with bipolar disorder. When I was happy, I was very happy. Everything in the world was perfect, and there was nothing that could go wrong. But when the low times hit, they were very low.

Once, I was in the shower and my mind just

wouldn't shut up. I was already in a depressed mood. As the steaming water caressed my skin, I couldn't help but think, "It's okay to leave your children, there are people here who will still love them." I was shaving my legs and brought the razor to my wrist. I let it dance there for a few minutes and then brought it to my neck. Tears formed in my eyes as I imagined warm, sticky relief running down my body. If only I had the courage to follow through, then all this pain can be released. I wouldn't have to wake up every day hating myself. It would all be over.

Then I began to hear Kylind, who was two months old at the time, cooing in his bassinet. I'm not sure if it was my mind trying to rescue me or if he really was trying to save my life. Either way, I knew I needed to fight these emotions and thoughts. It was not my time.

My husband and I were struggling financially before Kylind was born. We collectively had six children, supporting them all came with a challenge. I was just about to start nursing school when we learned I was pregnant for the fourth time. Our marriage turned sour because we were having many disagreements regarding having another child while already struggling. He wanted an abortion to happen; I didn't. I understood his personal reasons for thinking an abortion was the best choice, however I wasn't willing to, based on my religious beliefs.

I didn't believe in killing an unborn child. I believed that every life matters and if I had the abortion, I could never step foot in church again. I felt that I would be hated by God for killing a child. We remained at odds about the abortion for a while. I began to hate him for threatening me about it. "If you have that baby, you will raise it by yourself!". We remained at odds until one day I decided, financially, this was the best choice for myself and for our family.

I told myself everything would be okay the morning of the appointment. I had an uneasy feeling in my stomach, however; I knew what needed to be done. My best friend took me to the clinic and was my support person throughout the procedure.

When it came time to sit on the operating table, my hands became sweaty pools of anxiety. I was mentally talking myself into the confident person I needed to be to follow through with the procedure. Were they judging me? I thought, probably. I laid back on the table and let them prepare to start.

My mind began to race as the doctor instructed me to open my legs. She explained she was going to insert a needle to provide a numbing agent to help with the discomfort. My thoughts were getting louder and louder. As I felt a pinch within me, I sat up and said "No."

The doctor instructed me to lie back down because she had to continue the procedure. I repeated myself. "No." She signaled the nurse to go and get support. As I tried to stand up, four sets of hands pulled me back onto the table.

My heart felt like it was in my stomach. I began to scream and cry. I was scared. The medication in my system had me feeling too dizzy to put up much of a fight. I was pushed down and my hands were brought above my head, legs pried open.

Before I knew it, stabbing and scraping was all I felt inside of me. And it was over, I killed my son. Yes, I was far along enough to know that I was having a son and I had killed him. I went home that evening, hating everything within me.

That night, I went and sat in my bathroom. I searched the medicine cabinet for pills that were strong enough to get the job done. I was googling the pills I had and saw that the bottle of muscle relaxers was enough to at least leave me brain dead.

I emptied the bottle in my mouth, chewed them up, and went to swallow. I couldn't do it. I stood there looking at myself in the mirror. My skin was flushed and my hair was wild. The bitter taste in my mouth meant nothing. This was not how I was going to give up.

I spit them in the toilet and flushed. My story wasn't over. Not yet.

5

MISFORTUNE OF A BLACK GIRL

If there was ever a time to get into therapy, this was the time. Instead, my depression continued as I went through nursing school. I was pregnant again and married to who I realized was an alcoholic. Arguments became fights and boy, were they violent fights. Blood, bruises, and scars still remain on the consciousness of both of us. This was no longer a happy home.

"Every time I look at you and see that you're pregnant, I'm disappointed!" I'll never forget those words. My nursing friends never saw a frown on my face, but inside I felt I was dying. I hated the way I felt, but knew I had to finish school to end the financial dilemma we were facing.

As my belly grew, so did my depression. I wasn't prepared to go through sleepless nights and have to find babysitters all over again. I wasn't ready to look at how my body would change and the pain of labor. I was scared that my sadness would turn into postpartum depression as I had previously suffered from. Honestly, I just wasn't ready to do this all over again. So we considered adoption.

It seemed like the best choice for the both of us, because we were already in a bind. I was not over what happened to me during the abortion either. I felt guilty carrying another baby after I made the decision to get rid of one. Throughout the nine months, I tried not to get attached to the baby. I ignored when he kicked; I didn't sing or even rub my stomach. I wouldn't let other people touch me and I didn't talk about being pregnant. I just wanted to get through school and have the baby to get it over with.

I didn't even want to go to nursing school, but I had to do something to help alleviate the struggle we were facing with money. My husband had convinced me because he thought I'd make a good one. I knew I cared about people and my mother and grandmother were nurses, so I figured it couldn't be that bad. I took care of him after we were in a horrible car wreck about a year prior; I believed it made sense to just go ahead and obtain my nursing degree.

The accident was the worst thing in my life at the time. We were driving back home from a move we attempted down south. We learned that financial struggles will follow you wherever you move if you don't take care of them in the first place. So anyway, we came back. Family was there to help support the kids, so it was the only logical decision.

What we didn't expect was the move to almost cost us our lives. Two cars and three semi trucks were involved in a collision and our car was the first one that started the ripple effect. We hydroplaned and spun right into the intersection, which caused the first truck to slam into us, then the second, and a third.

I remember the whole thing like it happened yesterday. It was dark and wet, with glass and blood everywhere. I remember glancing in the back seat at my son and step daughters, praying they were going to make it out alive. Everyone was unconscious except me.

That night, I lost my husband. The man who

truly loved me died on the operating table when his heart stopped. They resuscitated him and the person I took home from the hospital to recover wasn't the man I fell in love with.

I took care of him every day; I bathed him and helped him with his physical therapy until he was strong enough to start doing a lot of his own self care. That's when he began to befriend a bottle of wine every night before joining me in bed. I grew lonely watching the person I loved lose himself to alcohol. This is when the nightmare started. I was reliving the night of the accident over and over. By the mornings, I'd wake up to a monster instead of my husband.

I started self silencing to avoid conflicts. I didn't enjoy fighting, but this didn't always work. Sometimes nothing worked. If he wanted to argue and fight, that's what we did. One night, I got up and left with the boys to avoid a fight. That next morning I came home to all the lights on in the house. I came to get a change of clothes. He was sitting at the top of the stairs.

The sight of him stopped me in my tracks. I wasn't sure if the alcohol was still in his system. I certainly was not ready for another fight. I gathered myself and walked past him, up the stairs, and to our bedroom. My back was turned as we began to argue. The next thing I know, my face went through the glass entertainment center in our room. I fell and managed to roll over. The shards of glass stung my face and back. I could taste salt and iron from my busted lip.

He had gotten on top of me and began to choke me. The room started to spin, and I whispered, "I'm sorry." It was all I could manage to say with the pressure of his hands closing in around my throat. Soon as he loosened his grip, I reached up and punched him in the face as hard as I could. It stunned him. He fell back, and I got up and ran. I jumped down the stairs and ran out of the house.

Later, a friend convinced me to go to the police station and file a complaint against him. I had cuts and bruises on my face. I was reluctant, but hopeful that maybe this would cause him to get the help that was needed to get us back on the right track.

I sat in the police station for two hours and no one came to take a statement or even checked on me to see if I needed anything while I waited. Everyone kept just walking by. I was already feeling embarrassed that I was even there in the first place, but to be ignored as well was adding insult to injury.

I got up and left. I went back home because that

was the only thing I knew to do at that point. By then, he was back to normal. This was the typical day for us, the routine that happened every so often. Sometimes family intervened, sometimes we were able to sort things out ourselves. Either way, this lifestyle was not healthy, and we both did not want our children becoming witness to this unhealthy parenting style.

One day we were arguing and something snapped in me. I had lost my temper and tackled him to the floor, and wrapped my hands around his neck. My thoughts were telling me "It's okay to kill him." So I kept my hands there. I just stared at him with so much hate. That was the scariest thing my mind has ever said to me. I let go finally and decided now was the time to seek help immediately.

Things were getting so bad. I was burning bridges with family and friends. I hated everyone, including myself. I never wanted so badly to be taken off this Earth. I had no outlet and no one to turn to that was willing to allow me to continue to abuse their efforts to help me.

I had refused to go to church for the fear that God would hate me for killing an unborn child. When I was stressed or needed words of prayer, church was where I sought tranquility. I had allowed myself to lose interest in the things I loved and the things around me. I saw no solution to climbing out of this dark serpentine I was falling through.

6

SHAMEFUL BLACK GIRL

I spent a lot of time angry at my father. I felt like if he was still active in my life, maybe I would not have gone through a lot of the things that I suffered. I held these emotions in and didn't speak about them much. I developed a self-loathing train of thought. I hated waking up every day to who I saw in the mirror. I didn't believe he truly loved me, his daughter.

We had a phone conversation once about how if I wanted to build a relationship with him; I had to put forth the effort. I had to make the calls and reach out to him to show him that I wanted him to be a part of my life. I couldn't even talk to him about boys, so how was I going to be able to open up to him and let him get to know me? I couldn't ask him questions or look for advice from him because it felt uncomfortable. I felt like I was pretending to be someone else with him. I only told him about good grades and sports. Instead of trying to build this impossible relationship with him, I spent most of my adolescent years trying to figure out things by myself. I stopped calling and reaching out. I got tired of searching for good things to talk about. The ratio of good to bad was growing on the negative end, and I wasn't comfortable sharing my experiences anymore. I started holding them in. Of course, we grew even further apart.

I felt unprotected in so many ways. I began to parent and protect myself. I didn't want anyone to see any signs of weakness within me, which started to make me feel lonely. A lot of my friends had both their parents growing up. To me, they always seemed truly happy, unlike the forced smile and serious look that was upon my face. They didn't feel the need to fit in like I did, they just belonged. The other girls in high school had friends and healthy relationships with everyone they knew. They were confident in their words and their looks. I was fearful of judgement, so I tried to make myself smaller. I didn't want people spending time with me outside of school because I feared that if they knew my secrets, they would use them against me. I second guessed and mistrusted anyone who wanted to get close to me. I was the one dealing with daddy issues. How could I truly trust a man would love me when my own father didn't?

I couldn't recognize when a guy truly liked me, and this made me begin to lose trust in myself. I was sad; I talked down about myself and even second guessed my decisions a lot. My confidence was low. I believed a lot of the misfortune that happened in my life was my fault; I had no reason to believe otherwise.

I thought about if I had someone to help me recognize when I was in unsafe situations or when someone wanted to take advantage of me. I felt that men were only interested in me for the wrong reasons, like sex. I began to feel unworthy of love. This was all a part of the negative thought patterns and the shame I felt from the trauma I had been through.

I never properly learned how to deal with trauma as a lot of black women alike. We would rather hide our shame. We hide and put defensive walls up. When something happens that we are not proud of, we instinctively tuck our pain away and save it for later. We didn't address it out loud, we just kept living life. After all, this is what we learned.

I mentioned before, I never saw my mother cry, but I knew when times were getting hard for us. She just kept her chin up. As an observer, I learned that this is how we deal with tough moments. We don't let it knock us down; we don't acknowledge it, we just find another way to keep going. Hiding from shame and embarrassment and only celebrating the good things that happened to us.

7

THE "STRONG" BLACK GIRL

I had spent years avoiding therapy. I had this made up idea that therapy was for the weak. Only those who can't handle life needed to cry about it to someone. How could someone who's never been through what I've suffered help me?

I battled my mind on whether what I had been through was even that bad. There are people on this earth who have had worse happen to them. I would often compare my life to those who were homeless or lost close family members and suddenly, my life was not so bad. These were the excuses I would use so I could convince myself that therapy was not needed. Looking back, they were also reasons that helped me stay strong and continue to push forward with life.

I often ask myself, why did I feel the need to be so strong? I had felt like I made so many mistakes in my life already that I needed to be the one to fix them by myself. I didn't need to ask for help. If I didn't have answers, I was going to find them on my own. I needed to make my parents see that I could be successful, and that I was not a failure. Yes, I already had three children, but I could finish school and start my career, too.

I needed to show everyone that I could make the impossible happen and I did not need any help to do it. Whether I stayed married or became divorced, I would be successful and not have to worry about my family being disappointed in me.

On the inside, I felt my world crumbling. This overwhelming feeling of hopelessness was always surrounding me. I began feeling like I would fail my children if I waited too long to get it together, that they wouldn't be proud of me. I was worried that I would be raising them to be failures, just like me.

I was literally living in fear. I have self conditioned to isolate and to shut off the outside world. I stopped going to the grocery store to shop. Too many people made me nervous. I stopped driving, afraid I would end up in a car collision. Things got so bad, I couldn't even work. My doctor had taken me out of work because I was shutting down.

A coworker of mine committed suicide just as I began working on my new unit. She was a little older than me at the time and had decided life wasn't worth living anymore. In the beginning, I often found myself crying for her because of the stories I had heard about how she was treated. I never met her but the way others talked about her when she wasn't working really hurt to hear. People bullied her even in death. It didn't feel good to be around those who felt the need to continue to dislike her, even after she was no longer alive. Her brother mentioned she left a note saying she was bullied and treated unfairly at work. I wish I had met her and wondered if I could have made a difference in Amanda's life. Her suicide increased my anxiety about working there. Was I going to be bullied to? I still think about her, she's another reason I had to be strong. I still visit her social media profiles from time to time. She reminds me, I'll be fine.

8

BOUNDARIES OF THE BLACK GIRL

"The things I would do to you if no one were around."

That's what he wrote to me in an unwanted love letter. I've wiped my memory of the details, but now and then pieces of it resurface from my unconscious mind. I was twelve, and he was sixteen. The letters were inappropriate and something more serious than an innocent crush. They were sexual and advancing.

I wrote back. I wrote things he wanted to hear, things that would make him happy. Even though I did not feel the same way, I said that I did. This continued for a summer. I was thankful when it was time for me to leave and return home.

I never found out what happened to those letters,

but I was relieved that it was over when it ended. I wanted to say how I really felt, that it was weird to me, that half the things written in those letters I didn't understand, anyway.

I wish I knew then how to set boundaries. I could have told him that this wasn't something that I was willing to accept. I could have spoken up and told my parents or his parents. Instead, I made things okay. I had no boundaries, and things were bound to keep happening as long as I allowed it.

Years later, I decided that I would try counseling and see what it had to offer me. A psychiatrist was also added to the list of things I needed to begin my recovering process. I had to really sit with myself and come to the realization that the bouts of depression, aggression, and suicidal ideation were not fitting for a healthy lifestyle. I did not want to raise my sons to be a product of an unhealthy environment. Problem solving did not mean solving with yelling or violence. So I decided that getting help was what I needed to do.

Learning what boundaries were and how to use them had to be my biggest struggle in therapy, if anyone ever asked. In my past, I wasn't provided with reasonable, safe guidelines. I didn't know how to enforce them when it came to others and how to respond if or when someone passed them. When something would happen, I found a way for life to just keep going.

The first thing I had to do was to acknowledge that the past was the past. The things that I had experienced were over with, and it was up to me to choose what I would do with the memory of it. I could live in it and let it forever haunt me or I could make these the reasons that I became a better version of myself. It was up to me to figure it out. This was the first boundary I had to set with myself. I had to accept that I couldn't change the past, but I could change my future. I didn't have to be angry all the time, and I didn't have to continue to beat myself up over it. This was my first step to healing. Acceptance.

It was time to recondition myself. I didn't realize that my mind had placed its own boundaries on me when I should have placed them on my mind. So I taught myself the phrase, "The mind is fear, the soul is free." It was the way I gained my power back. Thoughts live within the boundaries of the mind, they don't control the outside world. It was time to heal.

9

HEAL, BLACK GIRL

Being a strong black woman shouldn't be about the amount of pain you're able to endure, by pushing yourself to just "deal with it", it should be about saying "I'm strong enough to heal from what I've been through." We define strength in our own terms and we often hold ourselves to the standard of being a perfect woman. When we don't measure up to those expectations, we reject ourselves. We carry the weight of the expectations we haven't lived up to.

We chose to remain silent and strong. We continue to push forward and ignore our failures and shortcomings. By doing this, we reject and diminish our own sense of self because we ignore what we need at the time and do what must be done.

I can't tell you the amount of times I saw my mother put us, her children's needs, in front of her own. Rarely did I see her find ways to implement self care in her lifestyle. She was a hard worker and when she was home from work; she was a mother.

When children become adults, we often mimic the acts of our parents unless we know better. Once I became an adult, I spent most of my time working and being a mother. Those were the only two roles I knew about participating in. Lectures given to me about being a mother included the fact that there wouldn't be much time for me anymore. That life was all about my children. I believed that for a long time. I didn't know that I should still be continuing to plan small moments for myself to enjoy.

Having a baby at nineteen was looked down on by most of my family. So that also contributed to my postpartum depression. I listened to a lot of my family and they were disappointed in me. Mateo was five weeks old when I was sitting in a hospital bed. I was recovering from a transient ischemic brain injury. I remember as my uncle kissed me on my forehead; he whispered that I needed to make better decisions. I knew he was referring to me having a child at a young age.

I nodded my head in understanding. Another

blow to my self-esteem, that I now felt the desire to prove everyone wrong. So what if I'm a young mom, there's nothing wrong with me. I can still be a mother and live a good life. I can accomplish just as much as the next person. This set a fire ablaze within me. I can be a good mother and still be successful.

By now, I internalized more than enough pain. I was going to make my son proud of me, and that was all that had to matter to me. I was going to work hard and be the best mother that I could be. Mateo deserved it, after all. Although I was trying my hardest to stay on track in school, I found myself depressed and it was getting harder to stay interested in being a mom. I felt like Mateo needed to be with people who could love him better than I could. This is when I learned that I needed to begin my self-love journey, my journey to happiness.

I would often feel ashamed of the decisions I had made in the past and would allow my thoughts to center around them. I would silently be embarrassed. I would replay the situations and try to imagine different scenarios where the outcomes were better. I would talk negatively about how I felt about my choices, and it would ultimately turn into how I felt about myself.

I wanted all of my family to be proud of me for the decisions I made and to be proud of how I was living my life. I only reported the good things about my life to my father when we did talk and the rest of my secrets I would bottle up inside. I was afraid of being rejected by my family members, I wanted to make them proud of me. I was carrying the weight of my own expectations and theirs. Who was I really trying to prove myself to? I had this fear of rejection and was silently beginning to diminish my own self worth. I was still chasing the fulfillment of pleasing people. I knew it needed this to stop in order to truly be happy.

I desperately wanted to improve my internal image of self-worth and to be able to take care of myself without sacrificing for others anymore. Often, that's what the strong black woman would do, she would self sacrifice, and she didn't expect any form of reciprocation. She just did what she needed to do.

It was time to make a change. I was ready to stop living for those around me. I wanted to change the way I thought about myself and care less about what others had thought about me. I was ready to focus on my happiness, no longer looking for reasons to feel bad about myself. So I drew myself inward and began my counseling with no expectations.

While I was still shut off from the world, it was easy to say "no" because I had stopped answering the phone a long time ago, because of my own stress and anxiety. Someone only called me when they needed me to do something. I wanted to get rid of the disease to please people.

I started making a "to-do list" of five things to complete every day, the night before, as I went to bed. This included things like journaling, reading a chapter of a book, and spending time outside for at least thirty minutes a day. This was the start of me practicing self care. These activities started to become things that I enjoyed doing. I was looking forward to them daily.

In between that, my counselor wanted to work on retraining my brain. I had to get into the practice of observing my negative thoughts. At first, this was easy. I would write down the negative things that would come across my mind. We noticed that this would spark my anxiety to set in. Then she had me start evaluating each of the negative ideas. Were they true? Where did the thoughts come from?

The more I started doing the things that I wanted to do, I started to find small moments of joy coming back into my life. Self-care was sending me on the path to self healing. Self healing began to grow into self love.

I was reconnecting to who I was, I felt lighter in my heart and the smiles on my children's faces began to hold meaning to me again. I stopped making myself feel uncomfortable to please others, I started doing what I wanted to do without fear. I was truly getting to live the life that I was meant to.

Another part of healing was to forgive those who hurt me. I didn't say let go, but no longer feel angry or resent those who have caused profound pain in my life. I wanted to forgive so that I could continue on my journey of happiness and self-love. I needed to see that there are people with pure intentions still left in the world.

This is what led me to go on my journey of self-discovery. I needed to not only forgive others, but I needed to forgive myself for holding on to the pain for so long. So long that I was still blaming myself for things that happened to me when I was a child, as an adult. I wanted that inner voice that judged inside my mind to finally be silenced. I wanted to define myself on my own terms. Being free.

I needed to learn how to do that. So I began my research on self-discovery books. I would read as much as I could so that I could obtain as much information as I needed. I wanted to feel happy again, yes therapy was helping, but I also had to be willing to do more work outside of an hour session once a week. I needed to feel what it actually meant to feel "happy".

I had finally found books that helped me feel my childhood traumas and hardships I suffered years before. I had to sit with the emotions surrounding those memories. Sometimes I would journal about it, maybe even write a poem. Sometimes I sat and cried so hard I had a headache. Crying felt a hell of a lot better than anxiety hitting me so hard that I couldn't breathe. I wrote letters of forgiveness to myself and I taught myself to separate from the things I wrote in the letters. I trained my brain to think "I am not my trauma". I had to move forward. I couldn't thrive in the present while still living in my past. I wasn't enjoying my new career or the experiences within it. I had to make the change.

I journaled and spoke out about my pain. I gave advice to others when needed and when asked. I told my story in many ways to as many people who wanted to hear that it was okay to heal.

Many of us may feel like we have grown up with less than a perfect childhood, but if you're a mother, or planning to become a mother, I'm sure your goal is to give your children a better life than you had. One thing we often forget about while we are so busy with life is that we need to stop and heal. We need to recognize when we are neglecting ourselves, ignoring what we need. The only way to be the best parent is to become your best self.

This means we need to be better at recognizing when we are judging ourselves and using negative self talk to deal with a situation. Self love is about being kind to ourselves and forgiving ourselves for things that we didn't know before but know now. You have to trust yourself and choose yourself first.

Expression is the only way to let go of things that troubled me. Holding them in caused me to resent the very same things about me that I love now. I've been told that experience is the wisest teacher. We have to learn to forgive our younger self, believe in our current self and create the best version of your future self. It's time to heal, black girl.

10

LET THEM SEE YOU CRY

I think one of the most important things about being a mom and a woman is letting your children see you cry. Show them that it is okay with every emotion. We need to show them that emotions have reasons to be felt. We should show our children how to feel and address each emotion.

I didn't think adults cried until I became an adult. Boy, there were many times I wanted to cry, and I did not see that it was completely normal. Counseling played a huge role in allowing me to learn how to cry again. At first it felt weird, but I started to feel better after I cried. I felt a release.

I believe that the way we heal influences how we behave and respond to situations. Often growing up in a black household, I was told that children are to be heard and not seen. I took that and made myself as small as I could in a room. My feelings or thoughts didn't matter, and I definitely needed to stay out of "grown folks' conversations".

A lot of these conversations exposed me to things I should have learned about later in life. Topics I wanted to speak up about but was made to sit and act as though I weren't in the room. I believe this is why I didn't speak up about the suffering I went through as a child. I had lost my voice a long time ago.

Today, I use this voice that I have to speak up. No more experiencing depression and confusing it with failure. No more suffering in silence. No more preventing me from healing by obsessing over the past and how badly people hurt me.

I wasn't "fast" for wearing shorts and I will no longer feel ashamed of my body for how it developed. I will no longer accept the oversexualized comments from the older men of my past. I am the black girl who decides to change how she views herself. After all, her opinion is the only one that matters.

Black girl, let's heal the trauma that has been silenced by others in you. We have been raised in a society where we care more about other people's thoughts. We spend more time worrying about other people's thoughts and putting their perspective before our own. It's time to take our power back. Find what your own thoughts are, spend time with yourself, and get to know who you are. People will only have a version of you in their head that compliments their reality. This can be very damaging if you believe them. Therefore, you need to learn how to show up for yourself.

We all have habits to learn and unlearn. The only way to heal is to feel the things we have been through and let them go. This only allows us to move into the better version of yourself and, most importantly, break the cycle. Teach another black girl that she doesn't need to suffer in silence. Teach her to speak up when men don't respect our boundaries. Teach her ways to love herself and to be kind to herself when life doesn't happen as planned. Teach her to show up for herself. Let her learn to respect her own boundaries. You don't have to carry everyone else on your shoulders. It's not your responsibility.

So listen up, black girl, you don't have to be a strong black woman, be a healed one.

www.ingramcontent.com/pod-product-compliance
Lightning Source LLC
Chambersburg PA
CBHW060219050426
42446CB00013B/3117